NOT IN MY NAME

Alice Bartlett

NOT IN MY NAME

OBERON BOOKS
LONDON

First published in 2009 by Oberon Books Ltd
521 Caledonian Road, London N7 9RH
Tel: 020 7607 3637 / Fax: 020 7607 3629
e-mail: info@oberonbooks.com
www.oberonbooks.com

Cover image by Theatre Veritae from photographs by Seal Films
and Alice Bartlett: Jack Anwyl, Donna Rainford and Zahoor
Hussain performing in *Not in My Name*.

Visit www.oberonbooks.com to read more about all our books
and to buy them. You will also find features, author interviews and
news of any author events, and you can sign up for e-newsletters
so that you're always first to hear about our new releases.

CONTENTS

Introduction

When I agreed to write the play that became *Not in My Name* exactly two years ago, I had no idea of the extent to which this project would consume me. It began with a speculative approach from Andrew Raffle, a friend and former colleague, who appeared (although my mobile signal was particularly bad during our initial conversation) to be inviting me to develop young person-friendly script about terrorism.

Intrigued, and more than a little apprehensive, I attended a subsequent meeting with Andrew and Rozila Kana from the Lancashire Constabulary. The subject matter confirmed – to clarify the essential meaning of Islam for a diverse audience; to offer insight into the complex vulnerabilities surrounding extremist recruitment; to directly portray a terrorist atrocity in order to provoke cross-community debate – I questioned my suitability by declaring my ignorance. What right had I to write about such things? (And thought, but unexpressed: how could such a play be credibly performed by young people?)

An objective voice, I was assured, was what was needed. Though the play aspired to speak both with and for the local Muslim community, it was vital that it resonated much further. Misunderstanding of Islam is a widespread problem in our current society, it is not the exclusive premise of Muslims: many people have now been 'educated' about this religion by means of sensationalised inaccuracies passed on through mainstream media channels and some unpleasant political propaganda. We should all know that the vocal minority does not speak for the silent majority, and yet this is somehow so often assumed to be the case.

Essentially this is the deliberate emphasis of the title. The phrase is not uncommon – it was previously familiar to me as the slogan of the 'Stop the War' coalition in 2003, and has most recently been adopted by the 'Hope Not Hate' campaign – but evoked personal resonance when, while undertaking community research for the play, it was clear my appearance assumed my compliance with various dubious aspects of recent British foreign policy. It is unpleasant to be attacked because of how you look, for principles which you oppose, and furthermore to not be heard when you attempt to assert your dissent. Sadly the situation is not unique: an obvious, although more extreme, equation is with those many British Muslims who have become victims of racist attacks in their own country in the aftermath of 9/11 and 7/7. I hope that the title, and indeed the play, speaks for the too often silent majority.

A great many people contributed in many different ways to the creation of *Not in My Name*. They are too numerous to list here, and most of those I interviewed did not want to be subsequently recognised, but they know who they are and I am very grateful to them for their input and support. The first and second casts are credited individually; their role in developing the play was invaluable, both through their integrity in rehearsals and courage in performance. We initially had no idea of the enthusiasm with which our work would be received and, with the exception of Darren Kuppan (who was engaged as a 'professional mentor' for the first tour), all were young amateur actors, several making their stage debut at the time.

The play can be, and has been, performed by young people or (reasonably youthful looking) adult actors, although the notes that precede the play are intended primarily with those working with the former. Whilst no detailed suggestions for rehearsals are given, it is my opinion (perhaps inevitably, as the writer) that familiarity and confidence with the text should take precedence over theatrical effect – although if you have the time and resources to combine the two, so much the better.

With so many lines taken directly from actuality, the most effective performers are always likely to be those who convince us the words are their own. My own process of directing this play, with both young amateur and professional casts, has always emphasised the necessity for the actor to bring the experience of each character as truthfully towards themselves as possible: I have found it far less satisfying to construct performances around the traditional actor's notion of 'What if I was this person?' than to directly ask 'What if this had actually happened to me?'

The following section offers some ideas on starting work

around this play in a classroom or community environment, which I hope can be used alongside the script as a resource in its own right. Both Andrew and I have now seen the play resonate across many diverse communities – encompassing audiences of all ages and from many backgrounds – and continue to be inspired by proactive nature of the discussions it provokes, which are in some instances already facilitating positive changes at a local level.

The global threat of terrorism is a frightening prospect for almost everyone, and most of us feel helpless against it. Time and again throughout my research I knew I had touched a raw nerve: people wanted to talk about this, but many didn't know where to start, and were usually fearful of saying the wrong thing. Often the answer was to say nothing. And yet perhaps silence is dangerous too? By remaining silent: by not discussing what frightens us, or by not questioning what we don't understand, how can we start to address what is wrong? I hope this play might be useful to you in beginning such discussions. That is its intention.

Alice Bartlett, July 2009

Teachers' Resources

Many teachers and youth workers have already recognised *Not in My Name* as a valuable resource to begin positive discussions with young people around Preventing Violent Extremism (PVE) within or outside of the school curriculum. The following suggestions are taken from the resource pack accompanying Theatre Veritae's own production of the play, and assume no specialist drama knowledge as they are intended for cross-curricular application.

No one attempting to lead any of these exercises should feel the necessity to be an expert on the issues they relate to: all are based on the context of events that occur in the play, and the situations and opinions encountered within the play can be effectively used to frame your subsequent work. The activities are intended to be flexible, and most can be easily adapted to suit individual teaching styles and/or creative preferences. Most of the suggestions given here can be used either in isolation or as part of a more comprehensive programme.

Students should be familiar with the play before attempting these exercises, either through reading the script (individually or aloud in a group), watching the DVD, or from seeing – or even participating in – a live production. In most instances, we do not recommend using *Not in My Name* as a resource for young people under 14 years of age, due to the occasional use of graphic language and some potentially upsetting scenarios within it.

Beginning Conversations

These simple questions may focus students' thoughts before and after the play, also identifying immediate learning outcomes and relevant themes for subsequent exploration.

(1) Before students experience the play, whether through reading or watching, it may be informative to pose some simple questions regarding their expectations and to record their responses. For example:

- What do you think the play will be about?

- Do you have any questions that you hope the play will answer?
- What do you know about terrorism? Why does it happen?
- Who is affected by terrorism?

(2) It could be interesting to repeat these questions straight after the play, comparing responses in order to note changes in attitude, knowledge or opinion. Further immediate questions to extend reflection and discussion following the play could include:

- Could you relate to any of the characters?
- Did any of the information in the play surprise you?
- Have you learnt anything specific from the play?
- Has your opinion changed on anything?

Identifying the Victims

This exercise should be helpful in assisting students' recollection of a significant proportion of the play, as well as developing empathy with a range of affected characters and enhancing awareness of the wider consequences of Shahid's actions.

(1) Ask students to identify characters from the play who were affected by the attack either directly or indirectly. These should include characters whose voices are heard within the play, along with those who are mentioned but not directly portrayed.

(2) Perhaps as a character is mentioned, a student can stand within a presentation space to represent that figure; when working with larger groups, it may be helpful to write the character name on a sheet of paper for the student to hold.

(3) The group should then discuss who this character is or was: what is known of them from the play; what other details might be imagined of their life before the attack from the information given. Once a sense of this person has been established, the group should reflect on how that character was affected by the attack, which can be prompted by asking questions along the lines of:

- Where were they when it happened?
- How did they find out about it?

- What did they witness?
- What might they have felt at the time?
- Were they supported by anyone else?
- How possible is it to 'move on' after something like this?
- How has their life changed as a consequence of the attack?

(4) It is likely that students will easily identify the more obvious victims, including those who were physically harmed by the attack; they should then be encouraged to think beyond these individuals. We learn for example, towards the end of the play, that Assistant 2 remains unable to return to work despite being offered counselling; one of the girls, who saw badly injured bodies carried from the scene of the attack, has to remind her friends that:

GIRL 1: And we were in it too! I watched it all. I saw
  everything happen – when I was outside I saw
  everybody…coming out.

However she gives no indication of having received any comparable support. Victims of events that occurred as a consequence of the attack – such as the arrest of the family and tangible increase in local racial tensions – should also be considered.

As more characters are introduced and discussed, the extent of the personal impact across a whole community – encompassing both Muslim and non-Muslim figures – should quickly become apparent.

(4) Where there are relationships between the nominated characters, perhaps the students representing these people could reflect this by placing themselves either closer together or further apart as appropriate. It may then be worthwhile to compare the responses of these individuals, discussing how their respective behaviours may help or hinder the other characters.

What Really Happened?

It should be stressed that this exercise is not about apportioning blame for the attack – none of the characters could have known what would eventually happen – but rather about encouraging reflection on how small actions or responses can sometimes make a very big difference.

This activity is primarily based on the information discovered within the police interviews, recreated in the central section of the play. In this scene four characters share their observations of how Shahid changed over a period of time before his death. Some preparatory time should be spent re-reading or watching this scene with the entire class.

(1) The exercise can be undertaken either by individuals or in small groups, each of whom will be allocated one character from the scene to explore in more detail, either:

   a)   Shahid's brother
   b)   Shahid's younger sister
   c)   Shahid's girlfriend
   d)   Shahid's former best friend (the footballer)

(2) Each individual or group should attempt to identify the following:

   • What does this character say about their relationship with Shahid before he changed?
   • When and how did they notice that something was wrong?
   • What opportunities might this individual have had to intervene?
   • How could they have done this?
   • What are the factors that might have made saying or doing something difficult for this individual?
   • How might they have overcome these challenges?
   • Could this character have made a difference?
   • How does this person feel about Shahid now?

The script should be used as the starting point for this exploration, but does not contain all the answers. Students working in groups should be encouraged to discuss possibilities amongst themselves before presenting their findings to the rest of the class.

(3) It may be possible to link various groups' findings and suggestions to create a full timeline of events leading up to the attack, including possible points of intervention from the people who knew that something was wrong.

(4) Having examined these individuals in some detail, it is worth, if you have the time, broadening your discussion to encompass information heard in other parts of the play.

Several other young characters discuss their own relationship with and opinions of Shahid: returning to a similar set of questions, the group should investigate further when and how any of them might have been able to intervene.

Are there other people perhaps discussed but not represented within the play who could also have made a difference? For example, did Shahid make any attempts to discuss things that were troubling him? Might these have been handled differently?

All of these subsequent findings can also be incorporated within the timeline, which will hopefully by now illustrate a complex network of missed opportunities shared amongst various friends and acquaintances of Shahid.

Reporting or Distorting?

This activity has two distinct parts, which should both be completed. Students are encouraged to view the incident from different perspectives, developing their understanding of how to distinguish between accuracy, bias and sensationalism.

The starting point for this exercise is a moment in the play (which is not on the DVD) where some characters discuss the nature of the media reports on the attack:

ASIAN LAD 2: All the headlines seemed to say 'Muslims' or 'Islam'.

WHITE LAD 1: 'War on Terror gets Local'...

(1) Once again working either individually or in small groups, students can be asked to develop these news articles – either in

written, pictorial, recorded or dramatic format. The emphasis in the first part of this exercise is on creating the articles that students feel *would* have been written in response to Shahid's attack, rather than necessarily what *should* have been written.

Initially students should be encouraged to consider how many, or how few, of the actual facts would be available at the time of producing their article, and of the perspective their reporter might take. It should be assumed that the reporter is not from the community where the attack occurred, and has no direct link with any of the characters.

It may also be useful to ask:

- What is the intention of the report?
- Who is the intended audience?
- Who might have made themselves available for interview?
- How directly involved would that person (or people) have been in the incident itself?
- Do they represent a particular point of view?
- Is this endorsed or rejected by the reporter?
- Does the reporter choose to include everything they know about the incident in their article, or are certain pieces of information omitted?
- Does the reporter make any assumptions about the attack?
- Who or what might the reporter be particularly critical of?

(2) In sharing these reports it will be useful to highlight what is actually said, how this is said, and how these articles might make people who don't know anything about the attack feel. Do the students believe that the media are likely to help resolve the situation, or make it worse?

(3) Continuing this activity, students may either continue to work with their own report or swap with another group. They are now asked to read or view the article from the perspective of any character who has been directly involved in or affected by the attack. How would this person feel about the way the incident

has been reported? Are there any specific statements within the article that they might want to challenge or correct?

Students should prepare the responses of this character to the article, perhaps in the format of a letter to the newspaper, or a television interview. They will need to establish:

- Who they are and what their relationship to the incident is.

- What they have witnessed first-hand, and what information they have received from other sources (who they may or may not believe to be reliable).

- How the article has made them feel.

- How the article has been received within their community.

- Any specific information in the article that is perceived as inaccurate or even offensive.

- Why this is so, and how they would like to correct it.

- Anything else they would like the public to know about what has happened to them.

- How the media and public can best help their community to move on from this.

(4) To complete this activity, the initial report and response to it should be viewed side by side. Can any conclusions be drawn from these two perspectives? What particular aspects might students now be more aware of within press reports of real-life events, in order to distinguish between accuracy, bias and sensationalism?

Changing Attitudes

This exercise looks at the reactions and changing attitudes of a group of friends throughout the events of the play, and encourages students to explore how these characters could have better supported each other.

(1) Working in groups of four, students are asked to recall and explore the changing attitudes and relationships within the group of four girls, whose story frames the play. Beginning with four lines taken from different parts of the play, students are asked to create four still images (one for each line) that they feel

represents the relationship of these characters at the time the line is spoken:

a) 'We usually go into town on a Saturday.'

b) 'Please, please let me back in – my friends are still in there, I just need to know they're OK...'

c) 'I was sat on a bus and Kirsty wouldn't even sit with me.'

d) 'But I love Christmas – we have a Christmas dinner and everything in my family.'

(2) As each group shows back their images to the rest of the class, a discussion should take place around what is happening between the characters and how this relates to the wider events of the play. Students should be encouraged to examine what attitudes have changed within the group of friends and how this might have occurred:

- Why was it not possible for these characters to talk about the attack to each other earlier?

- Was the unkind behaviour meant, or influenced by other attitudes outside this group?

- Can the students imagine themselves being in a situation like this with their own friends?

- Do they understand why the fall-out occurred?

- When the images are negative, what advice might the students offer these characters to resolve the situation?

(3) It may be possible to create an alternate sequence of images, illustrating other options that this group of four friends could have used to deal with the events of the play without turning on each other.

Finding Out

A lack of understanding of a religious faith contributes to many of the problems within the play; this exercise compares the behaviour of two characters in order to help students assess the reliability of sometimes conflicting information.

(1) One of the initial criteria for commissioning the play was to address common misconceptions around Islam, which can be simply assessed after reading or watching *Not in My Name* by

asking two simple questions, both of which are directly answered within the play:

- What is the meaning of the word 'Islam'?
- What is the meaning of the word 'jihad'?

(2) With some groups, it may be beneficial to revisit the information provided about being a good Muslim in the play in more detail; many characters contribute to this discussion, but the most useful in terms of recapping will be statements made by the Brother, the Girlfriend, and the exploratory journey of the PCSO throughout the second half of the play.

(3) Although the information provided about Islam within the play is simplified, it is also accurate. Students wishing to explore this, or indeed any, religion in more detail should be encouraged to compare and contrast the experiences of Shahid and the PCSO:

- How did each of these characters of similar ages and from similar backgrounds apparently learn more about their faith?
- Which of these sources do students consider to be sensible and most likely to be accurate?
- Which of these sources do they feel should not necessarily be trusted and why?
- Which character did they feel understood more about his religion?

(4) Students should find a way of presenting their findings to advise other young people of reliable ways in which they can learn more about a specific religion; the play offers suggestions for finding out more about Islam, but this exercise can be used to address possible misconceptions around any major faith.

(5) Towards the end of the play, one character observes:

SPECIAL BRANCH: I find it sad that we never really hear about what the major faiths have in common – you know, everyone always focuses on the differences...

Asking students to highlight the main similarities between major faiths and belief systems can be a very positive exercise in demystification, as well as challenging preconceptions and supporting the development of mutual respect and understanding.

Points of View

A number of the problems that occur in the community after the attack are because of assumptions made about the reasons for the bombing and the kind of people who might have supported Shahid's actions. This exercise aims to develop empathy and understanding for individuals who feel judged because of wider attitudes towards a community they are seen as belonging to.

As explained in the introductory notes to the play, this is a verbatim text: meaning that although (unusually) the situation itself is hypothesised, many of the actual lines are taken from real conversations. This activity uses the following statements, which are all the honest responses of individuals discussing their own feelings about racism and violent extremism in Britain today:

a) 'I hope to God people don't expect me to apologise for his actions, because that's not my religion.'

b) 'They seem to think because you're this colour you're that religion. And it's not.'

c) 'Do you think I'm a terrorist? What makes you think that?'

d) 'We feel like we're going to get kicked out of England – and we've got nowhere to go 'cos we was born here and so was our parents...'

e) 'You get bad apples in every community, not just ours...'

(1) Ask students to individually choose one of these lines and consider who might have made this comment. In this instance it is not essential to use the characters from the play, although this is obviously still an option. Students should be encouraged to think about the possible background of this person, and what particular situations they might have encountered to precipitate this remark.

(2) It may be helpful to ask students to create a static pose that they feel represents how this person was feeling when they said

this line, and then to practise saying it themselves, experimenting with different attitudes until they find one that feels right.

(3) Students could also draw up a character chart in order to get to know their idea of this person better – a very simple way to do this would be to draw a spider diagram with each leg representing a different piece of information about the character; obviously there are no right or wrong answers here, as the development of this exercise is based entirely on supposition, but these kind of activities should support the students in developing empathy with the new character they are developing.

(4) Finally, ask students to write the line that they have chosen at the top of a blank piece of paper, and then to continue this into a stream of thought in the voice of the character – perhaps extending their responses to the initial statement or sharing other details of their life that may be connected to it.

(5) Students may wish to share or develop their work through performance, or through another art form with which they feel more comfortable. However often this exercise can stimulate very personal and thought-provoking responses; the activity of writing may be sufficient and some students may prefer not to immediately share their work aloud with the rest of their group or class.

Talking and Listening

Theatre Veritae's research with young audiences has found that Shahid is the character with whom students are most likely to identify; the reason usually given for this is empathy with the fact that no one in the play is really prepared to listen to him. We believe that this is an important finding, and this exercise aims to support discussion of how young people can ensure that their own voices are heard.

Following Theatre Veritae's production of *Not in My Name*, audiences have an opportunity to meet with an actor playing Shahid to correct his misconceptions about Islam, to hear his wider concerns, and to offer him advice that should prevent the events portrayed in the play from occurring.

Some indication is given in the play of the issues that were assumed to be troubling Shahid at the time of the attack, as well as some recollections of times when he attempted, but failed, to put his point of view across. Although no one in the play knows for certain why Shahid acted in the way he did, the assumption can be made that a whole range of factors combined over time to bring him to this desperate point.

(1) Audiences are usually asked after our own production to consider *who* should be listening to Shahid's various concerns, as well as *what* non-confrontational means Shahid might use to approach these people; these questions can be easily translated to a classroom setting.

(2) It might also be constructive to ask students to consider their own area, and the range of services and adults that may be available for someone such as Shahid to speak with either confidentially or in a group environment. Perhaps, after undertaking further research, they could create a map of such provision and how to access it within their own community.

(3) To complete this activity, students should be asked to 'make a wish': that is, to each nominate one simple 'action' or 'notion' that they feel might help reduce current problems relating to the presence of violent extremism and threat of terrorism within our society. Students should be encouraged to consider positive actions that can be achieved at a personal or local level rather than addressing more complex global problems.

The 'wishes' precipitated by this could be collected and recorded in a number of different ways; here are some suggestions:

- On post-it notes and placed on a larger poster.
- On paper leaves and tied to a potted tree.
- Collected verbally and recorded on film or using an audio device.
- As part of a visual mosaic or collage.
- Through text messages to a school mobile or intranet.

(4) The idea of this activity is to provide a positive platform for students' voices to be heard. However you choose to record the thoughts and suggestions of students, if you feel they have

responded with integrity, please give some consideration to what else might be done with the finished piece of work:

- Have they made any suggestions that might be of value to your school management team?
- Or to any local authorities?
- Or perhaps to someone with a national remit?

Essentially, if you believe your students have something valuable to contribute to this ongoing social debate, how can you support them in doing so?

Wider Responses

This activity, which could be completed individually or in groups, offers students an opportunity to creatively express and communicate their reactions to seeing or reading the play through a format chosen by themselves.

This could take the form of creative writing, for example: a play review, such as we see in newspapers; the diary recollections of one of the characters; a short story, poetry or rap.

It could be a visual arts exercise; perhaps a drawing, painting, collage or sculpture which may or may not use text from the play. It could be graffiti.

It could be a short, devised presentation or play. Or something dance-based.

It might be musical (with or without words) and could be in any style: maybe hip-hop or metal or bhangra or grunge.

However the students choose to present their response, they should be encouraged to honestly consider and try to portray the following within their work:

- What they feel is the central message of *Not in My Name*.
- Any specific issues that the play has encouraged them to think more about.
- Their attitudes towards the presence of violent extremism and continued threat of terrorism within our society.
- How they feel these issues are (or aren't) being dealt with at the moment.

- Their own visions for addressing these or related problems.

This work can then be captured and exhibited by live and recorded means and perhaps also presented to other groups, including students through a school assembly, or parents and key representatives from the wider community. If appropriate it could also feature on school websites, or in local newsletters.

And please remember, Theatre Veritae would also be very pleased to receive your feedback and examples of your students' responses to these or any other activities related to *Not in My Name* at info@theatreveritae.com.

Some Notes on the Play

This play was written with and for a young cast, aged from their early teens up to their mid-twenties, and all the characters can fall within this age bracket. The multi-role playing element is optional and could be worked in a number of ways, with the possibility of using as few as eight actors or more than thirty. Some characters are gender-specific and some are ethnically-specific (although this will inevitably vary in different parts of the country); others are interchangeable in the hope of providing a degree of casting flexibility.

It is, of course, quite possible for *Not in My Name* to be performed by groups whose own ethnic or gender balance does not align precisely with a naturalistic reading of the script. Indeed if the play is intended primarily as a vehicle for class discussion, it may prove constructive to allocate roles against expectation, allowing students more opportunity to identify with perspectives that may initially be perceived as alternate to their own. If the play is subsequently to be performed to a wider audience, then specific representational choices can be simply communicated through a clear and appropriate production concept.

The absence of fully comprehensive character breakdowns, either within the play or its supporting material, is intentional. Those details which are included are clearly important and should be adhered to, but it is hoped that any actor will also find considerable scope to make each part his or her own.

The original cast credits within this script provide some suggestion of role combinations that have previously proved successful, although there will of course be other possibilities. (It should also be noted that the development of Assistant 2 in the second half of the play was not incorporated into the original productions.) Thirty speaking parts are listed in order of appearance, ranging from those with just a few lines to some very substantial roles, the combination of which can hopefully offer performance opportunities for mixed groups of young people with varying degrees of dramatic experience, ability and confidence.

For larger and more adventurous groups, a number of scenes also have the potential to incorporate significant numbers of non-speaking characters – examples of this would include the action both within and outside of the supermarket; the busy Accident and Emergency ward of the hospital; the street rioting and its immediate aftermath – all of which, if carefully choreographed, can only enhance the degree of theatrical challenge, innovation and impact.

It is important to stress that there is no central character: *Not in My Name* tells the story of an entire community pulling apart before coming together through a period of extreme crisis, and as such must be viewed as an ensemble piece within which every voice, no matter how great or small, is vital to the overall montage.

CONTENT AND STYLE

This is a verbatim play in that many of the words used and concerns raised are those of a wide cross-section of people who agreed to be interviewed as part of an extensive research period, sometimes extended by additional accounts available within the public domain. Many viewpoints are represented: inevitably some of these are contradictory and others offensive; the occasional brutality of the language and more graphic illustrations of horror are necessary components to a play that takes the representation and aftermath of a terrorist atrocity as its central theme and should not be diluted in performance unless essential.

However, while the issues are current, and the opinions and indeed many eye-witness details are real, *Not in My Name* varies from most verbatim scripts in that it is a story: a hypothesis of what *might* occur in the event and aftermath of a localised terror attack rather than a reconstruction purposefully based upon any previous disaster. As such, it is told as a cautionary tale in the hope of addressing some common misconceptions around Islam and terrorism, and stimulating meaningful discussion and debate around these and other issues relating to the prevention of dangerous or violent extremism – which is not in this country at the present time purely a concern over Islamic fundamentalism.

The play is intentionally anti-climactic, concerning itself with consequences rather than sensationalism, and performers are encouraged to apply this note to their own interpretations: over-dramatisation, particularly in the earlier stages of the play, may quickly lead to melodrama. It will be observed that much of the language is retrospective, and can be played directly to the audience; rarely is the fourth wall necessary, or indeed desirable, in *Not in My Name*.

Watching the television news can be a useful exercise in gauging an appropriate manner of delivery: survivors from the midst of extreme trauma seldom speak with any great animation in its aftermath; the residue of real terror is conveyed not through what is said, but by the unfilled silences where words are simply inadequate. It is hoped that most performers attempting this play will personally have no directly comparable experience from which to draw; their portrayal is likely to come closest to the verbatim truth if it is based not on imitation or assumption, but on empathy and compassion.

SETTING

The play is set in a small town somewhere in the North of England, although with minimal adaptation it could be anywhere within the United Kingdom and perhaps beyond. It should be acknowledged that this version of the script was developed in East Lancashire and as such is representative of a specific local demographic.

At the time of publication, developmental work will have started on forthcoming productions in other areas – including a cosmopolitan city and a former mining community – and anyone interested in producing *Not in My Name* or developing their own programme of work around it is welcome to discuss any locally appropriate alterations with either Alice or Andrew at Theatre Veritae (info@theatreveritae.com).

The set itself needs to encompass a variety of locations and should support the fluidity of the story telling. There is no need for this to be either literal or expensive, and it is likely that simpler solutions will prove more creatively satisfying. Exploration with available lighting resources should obviously greatly enhance the theatrical impact of any production, along with attention to the details of sound design – be these realistic, abstract or musical – that might more effectively layer an acoustic backdrop to the spoken words.

The action should always feel as though it is taking place in the present and if particular details become outdated, with particular emphasis on any developments in terror legislation or new world events, then these should be amended. The date given on the first line and in the final speech is the day before Mother's Day of the following year.

Characters

GIRLFRIEND	SISTER
GIRL 1	FRIEND
GIRL 2	TEAM MATE
GIRL 3	NURSE*
FOOTBALLER	FEMALE SBO
MANAGER	WPC 1*
SON	WPC 2*
ASSISTANT 1	INNIT BOY
ASSISTANT 2	WHITE LAD 1*
SBO*	WHITE LAD 2*
PCSO*	ASIAN LAD 1*
ASIAN TEEN*	ASIAN LAD 2*
WHITE TEEN*	WHITE LAD 3*
COLLEAGUE	MUSLIM
BROTHER	ATHEIST

* These characters all have the potential to be sub-divided if working with:
- (a) larger casts, where more roles are required.
- (b) smaller casts, if exploring feasible multi-role playing options.

It should however be noted that the SBO (Special Branch Officer) should ideally be played by a white actor in the penultimate scene of the play; also that the PCSO (Police Community Support Officer) should be played by only one actor throughout the second half of the play.

The play also provides a number of opportunities to involve further groups of non-speaking characters within particular scenes if desired: this is explored in more detail in the introductory notes on the play.

Not in My Name was first performed at Burnley Youth Theatre 23 April 2008 with the following cast:

SON,   Imtannaan Abas
GIRLFRIEND / FRIEND,   Safia Anwar Ume
ASSISTANT 1 / WHITE LAD 2 / ATHEIST,
    Jack Anwyl
MANAGER / SPECIAL BRANCH OFFICER /
COLLEAGUE / TEAM MATE / WHITE LAD 3,
    Shaun Foxcroft
POLICE COMMUNITY SUPPORT OFFICER /
    INNIT BOY / ASIAN LAD 1,   Zahoor Hussain
SISTER / MUSLIM,   Bushra Irshad
FOOTBALLER / ASSISTANT 3 / WHITE TEEN /
    WHITE LAD 1,   Jamie McGowan
GIRL 1 / NURSE,   Donna Rainford
ASSISTANT 2 / WPC,   Gaby Mott
GIRL 2 / WPC 2,   Steph Shaw
ASIAN TEEN / BROTHER /
    ASIAN LAD 2,   Mohammed Owais
GIRL 3 / FEMALE SPECIAL BRANCH OFFICER,
    Pakeezah Younis

Director Alice Bartlett
Designer Jonny Quick
Project Management Kyra Milnes &
    Andrew Raffle
Production Assistants (Youth Theatre) Alex Bailey &
    Mariam Yousaf
Forum Emily Bowman & Jag Sanghera
Administrator Gareth Davies
For Lancashire Constabulary Rozila Kana

Not in My Name was subsequently revised for a touring production, also directed by Alice Bartlett, 1 September 2008 with the following cast:

MANAGER / ASSISTANT 1 / SPECIAL BRANCH
OFFICER 2 / WHITE LAD 1 /
    ATHEIST,   Craig Bennett
FOOTBALLER / ASSISTANT 2 / SPECIAL
    BRANCH OFFICER 1 / WHITE LAD 2,
    Shaun Foxcroft
SON / POLICE COMMUNITY
    SUPPORT OFFICER 2 / INNIT BOY /
    ASIAN LAD 2,   Zahoor Hussain
GIRL 3 / SISTER,   Madeeha Imtiaz
POLICE COMMUNITY SUPPORT OFFICER 1 /
    BROTHER / ASIAN LAD 1 / MUSLIM,
    Darren Kuppan
GIRL 2 / WPC 2,   Anna Marsland
GIRL 1 / WHITE TEEN / NURSE / WPC 3,
    Donna Rainford
GIRLFRIEND / FRIEND / ASIAN TEEN /
    FEMALE SPECIAL BRANCH OFFICER /
    WPC 1,   Lina Sultana

Not in My Name was commissioned by the Lancashire Constabulary in response to an identified need for young people to be able to discuss current issues around terrorism and extremism in an informed and proactive manner.

Theatre Veritae would like to particularly thank the following organisations who have previously contributed to the development of *Not in My Name:*

A donation from the royalities of this play will be made to the charity Victim Support, in particular recognition of their work supporting victims of terrorist attrocity and hate crime.

Further information on Victim Support, including full details on getting their help, can be found at
www.victimsupport.org.uk

Saturday morning.

The four GIRLS are friends from college. They begin their weekend routine in their separate homes.

GIRLFRIEND: It was Saturday 13th March.

GIRL 1: I got up late 'cos I was tired from Friday.

GIRLFRIEND: I remember the date 'cos it was exactly a month after my birthday.

GIRL 2: Saturdays, Mum lets me have breakfast in bed.

GIRL 3: I was watching The Disney Channel. *High School Musical 2.*

GIRLFRIEND: It was a really nice day.

GIRL 1: I phoned round my mates and said:

Wanna go shopping in town?

GIRL 3: Yeah, I need to get some make-up. But I mustn't spend much 'cos I'm saving for some boots…

GIRL 2: I can't, I've gotta work.

GIRL 1: I thought you worked Sundays?

GIRL 2: I swapped, just the afternoon – we're taking Mum for lunch tomorrow.

GIRL 1: Shit! I'd forgot! I need to get a card an' all.

GIRL 3: Are you coming, Safa?

GIRLFRIEND: I don't feel like it. Me and Shahid had a row last night.

GIRL 2: What about?

GIRLFRIEND: Same as usual. He's just being really weird at the moment.

GIRL 1: I think you should dump him.

GIRLFRIEND: I can't.

GIRL 3: Why not?

GIRLFRIEND: 'Cos I love him.

GIRLS 1, 2 & 3: Right...

GIRLFRIEND: I'm gonna call him in a bit. Maybe we'll hook up later?

GIRL 2: I'll text you all when I'm done.

GIRL 1: A'ishah, when d'you wanna meet?

GIRL 3: A couple of hours? I've gotta get changed... Same place as usual?

GIRL 1: Yeah, sorted. See you in a bit.

GIRLS 2&3: See ya.

The GIRLFRIEND is left alone.

GIRLFRIEND: We usually go into town on a Saturday. Sometimes just me and him, sometimes with all my mates as well. But the night before he'd said that we weren't to go town today. He never used to tell me what to do like that...

I called his phone but it was off so I left a message. Then I just went back to bed and watched TV.

The FOOTBALLER is warming up.

FOOTBALLER: I'd been told that morning I was making my first team debut. And not just in the squad, the gaffer had said:

MANAGER: (*Scottish accent.*) You'll be in the starting line-up. 'Cos of injuries and that.

FOOTBALLER: I was nervous, yeah, but dead excited – the stakes couldn't have been higher.

MANAGER: We need to keep up the pressure for the title.

FOOTBALLER: Had to make a good impression...

MANAGER: A local derby's no excuse to drop points.

FOOTBALLER: I could already see the headlines: 'The new Rooney'... 'United 5, City 0'...

We were gonna stuff 'em!

The SON enters, pushing a shopping trolley. He looks very young.

SON: Mum does a big shop every Saturday. There's a lot of us, and that's when she buys our food and that for the week. I'm always expected to help, 'cos I'm the oldest. Sometimes I try and think of some excuse not to go – but with the baby coming, it's not fair for her to be on her own.

And I needed to get a present from us all. 364 days she does everything for the family, and we've got that one special day to give her something back. So I said I'd go along with her.

Inside the supermarket.

ASSISTANT 1: I'd had a late lunch break and when I got back they said I was greeting people. Which is alright, it's dead easy – you just like say 'Hello' when people come into the shop, ask if there's anything you can help them with, that sort of thing... And if one of your mates comes in, you can have a bit of a chat.

GIRL 2: You can't do that if you're on the checkouts – if you're dealing with a customer, all your attention's supposed to be on that customer.

GIRL 1: All the Mother's Day stuff was on a stand at the front of the store.

GIRL 3: Cards, flowers, toiletries...it was all there.

SON: I wanted to get something I could hide in my coat pocket, so she wouldn't know I'd bought it.

ASSISTANT 1: When Shahid came in he was carrying this big sports holdall with Man United on it. It didn't seem odd because he was really into his football when we were at school. We were in the same year and had had quite a few classes together, but we'd not kept in touch since.

GIRL 3: I chose a card and a little bottle of lavender bubble bath, which is Mum's favourite.

GIRL 1: I didn't know what to get…

ASSISTANT 1: I think he was a bit surprised to see me, it being, like, out of context. Then he basically said to come with him because he had something to tell me.

SON: I waited until we were in the middle of the store near all the household stuff, then I said I needed to go to the toilet. She said she'd wait for me in that aisle, and I went off to get her present.

ASSISTANT 1: Now it's alright to leave the door for a few minutes if a customer asks you – usually they want you to show them where something is or something like that…

GIRL 3: Kirsty was faffing about, so I just said:

Wait for me here, I need to get some make-up.

GIRL 1: Fine.

ASSISTANT 1: We went over to an aisle in the middle of the store, where all the bleaches and lighter fluids and stuff like that are.

And then he told me he had a bomb.

ASSISTANT 2: I was stacking shelves on that aisle when it all kicked off.

ASSISTANT 1: I froze for a second and just thought 'Oh my God'. You just get that panic – you just start panicking and you don't know what to do. It didn't feel real… Why here? Why me?

ASSISTANT 2: We haven't had training to deal with stuff like that.

GIRL 3: The make-up and that's right at the other end of the store. I was on my way there when I heard a bit of a disturbance.

GIRL 2: I could see from my till there was something going on.

ASSISTANT 1: He said some words I didn't understand...

GIRL 3: I tend to ignore that sort of situation. It sounded like there was some Arabic which might have been from the Koran, but I don't really know.

ASSISTANT 2: I thought 'What's wrong with him? What the hell is he talking about?'

ASSISTANT 1: I know it's clichéd, but there was something about Iraq and his jihad against the West... I mean, what do you say to that?

GIRL 3: I just find it really embarrassing when you hear people going on with all that extreme stuff in public.

GIRL 2: On the check outs – basically every desk where there's a till – there's also a panic button underneath.

GIRL 3: I mean, no normal Muslim would say things like that.

GIRL 2: I pressed the button.

ASSISTANT 1: A couple of other people came over and tried to talk to him.

ASSISTANT 2: The only thing you're told is if there's a disaster – floods or bombs or anything like that – you're to ring the Disaster Helpline that's on the back of our badge.

Only I've got a new badge, and it's not on mine...

GIRL 2: My supervisor came over and saw what was happening.

GIRL 3: I looked at the guy and realised it was Shahid.

ASSISTANT 1: He was getting really angry.

GIRL 3: I was just so shocked, because I didn't think he was like that.

ASSISTANT 2: I thought I'd better go and get some help...

GIRL 3: I thought, you know, what do I do?

ASSISTANT 1: I don't know, I was just so frightened – my head was all over the place.

GIRL 2: You're supposed to reassure people that everything's alright, even though it was blatantly obvious that it wasn't – it was right in front of me, so I couldn't get out of it.

GIRL 3: I thought 'I know him – maybe I can help...'

GIRL 2: I know some cashiers lied and said it must be a false alarm or some sort of training exercise.

ASSISTANT 2: My supervisor said we was going to sweep the shop floor – except that area – and basically get just everyone out as quick as we could, but without causing a disturbance.

GIRL 2: I just had to say to people:

Stay calm, it will be alright. We've got security here...

I was really worried though.

GIRL 3: I just stood there... I didn't know what to do.

ASSISTANT 2: 'Cos I'm new I just had to get people out by the entrance. Most of the others started from the back of the store.

GIRL 3: There was already some people trying to calm him down – one of the shop assistants, an Asian lady who was quite heavily pregnant, and a couple of others.

ASSISTANT 1: I remember saying:

There's mothers and children here – can I get some people out?

You do feel that. I don't know where it stems from really…

Back at the entrance.

GIRL 1: I was just waiting for A'ishah when this guy comes over and was like:

ASSISTANT 2: I'm afraid I'm gonna have to ask you to leave.

GIRL 1: What? I haven't done anything! I'm just waiting here for my friend…

SON: What's going on?

ASSISTANT 2: Look, don't make a fuss. Everything's alright, it's just we need to get everyone out. You can wait for your friend outside…

GIRL 1: He was polite to us, although I did think at the time he looked quite scared.

She leaves.

SON: I said:

No, I need to get back to my Mum – she's waiting for me over there…

He runs back into the store.

ASSISTANT 2: I felt bad but I let him go – 'cos I just wanted to get out of there.

ASSISTANT 2 leaves.

ASSISTANT 1: And it was like – I suddenly realised that was it, there were no going back, he was definitely gonna do it…

GIRL 3: I shouted over:

Shahid, what's going on?

ASSISTANT 1: I'm not proud of this, but I turned and ran and shouted at everyone that were in my way:

Just get out as quick as you can!

GIRL 2: It was clear something had happened. People suddenly started to panic and there was some screaming.

ASSISTANT 1: I was acting under pressure, because obviously it just takes the flick of a button don't it. And you're gone straight away –

GIRL 3: That's when he did it.

A stark lighting change.

SON: There was a really loud bang.

GIRL 2: The blast was huge.

ASSISTANT 1: And suddenly, it's like you're in a different place.

SON: People were flying all around. Arms and legs.

GIRL 2: Everything was off the shelves.

GIRL 3: Body parts. Bits of body parts…

SON: There was glass everywhere.

ASSISTANT 1: And there was lots of blood.

GIRL 3: And there was huge amounts of screaming.

GIRL 2: You might think you've heard screaming…you've not heard that kind of screaming.

ASSISTANT 1: It was unnatural.

SON: It was unreal.

GIRL 2: This was the screaming of seriously injured, dying people.

GIRL 3: Frantic screams.

SON: Desperate screams.

GIRL 3: And then you're left with just a few people screaming.

ASSISTANT 1: Some people crying out quietly.

SON: A mobile phone, which no one answered.

GIRL 2: And then silence.

SON: And then it started to rain.

ASSISTANT 1: I think those sprinkler things had come on.

GIRL 3: It's weird, but the water was actually quite calming.

GIRL 2: There was no panic because you were still alive, even though you knew that other people probably weren't alive.

SON: But all around…it was horrible.

ASSISTANT 1: It was like a scene from hell.

GIRL 2: There was carnage everywhere.

SON: There was one man with really bad head and chest injuries, and a young child with a nail sticking out of her cheek.

GIRL 2: You think: 'Is there anyone I can save here or take out with me?'

SON: The child looked about six or seven. She was just very, very shocked.

GIRL 3: It felt like I was sinking…

ASSISTANT 1: There was something on top of me.

GIRL 3: 'Close your eyes, everything will be alright, someone will find you…'

ASSISTANT 1: I tried to shift it and it was a body, half a body… a dying body.

GIRL 3: Everything went, like – kind of very, very muffled.

GIRL 2: I became aware of this massive bleeding gash full of glass in my wrist – I looked and I could actually see the bone…

Then I felt sick.

ASSISTANT 1: I was underneath a dying body.

SON: I shouted out:

Mum, where are you?

GIRL 2: I was lucky. One person on the floor – I think it was a woman – was trying to get up, but she had lost one of her arms and both legs.

It was literally like looking at an anatomy picture of inside of the human body. I wanted to help, but…

GIRL 3: I was fighting against blacking out, knowing that if I did that I wouldn't come out from it.

ASSISTANT 1: I suddenly panicked:

Why does no one come? Does anyone know we're here?

GIRL 2: She was never going to make it.

SON: I started to cry. I still feel emotional talking about it now, y'know.

GIRL 3: I just said to myself:

I'm not going to die here – this is not the end of my story.

Outside the supermarket.

POLICE are cordoning off the area.

SPECIAL BRANCH: The initial call went straight through to the emergency services. We set up our own special command unit inside headquarters, giving us a central point in order to co-ordinate the response with all the other emergency services and the army.

Invariably in an incident of this nature, the police and emergency responders don't go straight to the scene as further devices may still be detonated.

So, yes, there would have been victims there that were not initially attended to as they couldn't make it to the first responders – which came as a big shock to people really.

GIRL 1: I was maybe fifty feet from the entrance – that was all. I think it hadn't quite sunk in. It's the kind of thing where you see it on the news, but don't expect to be in it. And I was in it, and it was horrible.

PCSO: The message came through on the police radios. It was pretty chaotic at first, as you would expect. There were blast injuries, and a lot of people were traumatised. Once an area was cordoned off, my job was to keep people behind that.

GIRL 1: I knew what it was straight away. Literally there'd been this huge 'boom' inside, and then the smell of an explosion with it...

SPECIAL BRANCH: There was an inner cordon – about 400 yards – and an outer cordon, which covered most of the town centre really. The emergency services sat just inside the inner cordon and there was restricted access to people from the outer cordon, so we checked who was going in and out.

GIRL 1: Everyone was absolutely terrified. I mean, there was smoke everywhere – I don't think there was a fire, but there was loads of smoke. People were still trying to get out, and you could see lots of them had been injured – there were people with blood all over their faces, someone had loads of cuts – and then we heard that someone had died.

PCSO: We have to reassure the public – try and keep people calm, take details of witnesses and that. It's a difficult role because we have to speak to the victims, speak to the people that are concerned or the people that have actually been affected by it.

GIRL 1: I just said:

Please, please let me back in – my friends are still in there, I just need to know they're OK…

PCSO: What are their names? D'you know what they're wearing?

We take all that detail and feed it into the system, so by speaking to everyone we managed to get a lot of people together, rather than have that person panicking at all hours or going to the police station.

A crowd has started to gather.

SPECIAL BRANCH: One of the first things we did was to set up, through the radio, announcements and updates initially about what the situation was, and also an emergency line that people could contact because there was obviously a whole state of confusion.

PCSO: I mean, at that point no one really knew what had happened, but already the rumours had started…

ASIAN TEEN: What? Suicide bomber?

WHITE TEEN: Bet it was them fuckin' Pakis!

PCSO: It's just one of them things – people have that mentality and you can't take it away from them. I heard some Asian kids saying:

ASIAN TEEN: So what, it's our Holy Book, innit? It's alright what he's done.

PCSO: And the white kids were giving me a hard time 'cos they'd heard it was an Asian person that had done it:

WHITE TEEN: I ain't speaking to you – you're all the same. It was your bro just killed my cousin.

PCSO: And I challenged them, I said:

Don't look at my colour, look at what I'm wearing. I understand you're upset, but so am I – 'cos I'm British just as much as you are.

And then I heard someone say:

ASIAN TEEN: Have yous heard this fuckin' coconut!

PCSO: I didn't get it at the time... It was only later when I told another officer:

COLLEAGUE: Well, what is a coconut?

PCSO: I dunno. Bounty. What're you on about?

COLLEAGUE: What colour is it?

PCSO: Er, brown.

COLLEAGUE: And on the inside?

PCSO: White.

And I thought, 'Oh my God, is that what they meant? Brown on the outside, white on the inside...'

Why? Why say that? I'm not here because I'm Asian and the bomber was Asian – I'm here because I'm a PCSO. And I'm just trying to do my job.

In three separate locations.

BROTHER: We got a call quite early on.

SISTER: One of my friends had seen him go in there a few minutes before the explosion.

BROTHER: She obviously knew when it happened/

SISTER: / This was before it were on the news –

BROTHER: And thought:

FRIEND: I think Hana's brother's in there, I've got to let her know...

BROTHER: Straight off I called his mobile, which was off.

SISTER: Hasan left a message.

BROTHER: I just said:

> Hey bro, I know we ain't been seeing eye to eye on stuff lately, but please call home and let us know you're safe. 'Cos sommat's happened in the town centre, and we think you might have been near there, and…we're praying you've not got hurt.

GIRLFRIEND: It came on the TV – one of those news alerts interrupting the normal programmes. As soon as I see something like that my first thought is 'Please God, don't let it be a suicide bomber.' It does actually come down to 'Please God, don't let him be Asian'.

> Then I realised where it was… Didn't know that facts, didn't know anything at all – no one did at that stage – all I could think about was my friends…

> And when the sirens you can hear on the news are actually going past your door…that's a whole new thing.

FOOTBALLER: They say bad things come in threes. I played like crap and got subbed at half-time, City have done the double and already everyone's blaming team selection; then one of the lads says:

TEAM MATE: Have you heard the news?

FOOTBALLER: And it was like…what the hell's going on?

> I mean, you're always shocked when that sort of thing happens, but it's just a little town – it's not even like it's in Manchester…

SISTER: Mum and Dad weren't talking.

BROTHER: We had it on the TV. It looked so bad…

SISTER: What was there to say?

> (*To family.*) I'm sure he's alright – he's always leaving his phone off.

FOOTBALLER: I was ringing round my family and all my mates to check everyone were OK, but a lot of the lines were jammed 'cos obviously a lot of other people were trying to get through as well.

BROTHER: When the number came up for friends and relatives I rang that:

NURSE: I'm afraid we've no record of him at the moment, but we're still logging the casualties. I know it's hard, but please don't come to the hospital unless we let you know he's here…

GIRLFRIEND: I couldn't get through to anyone, but there was this emergency number they were giving out on the TV that you could phone if you knew or thought you knew someone that might be there.

They were really good – I gave the names of my friends and they were already in the system:

NURSE: They were close to the blast, and your friend's condition is serious. But we're doing everything we can for her… I'm sure she'll be OK.

FOOTBALLER: I didn't call Shahid, I didn't even think of him to be honest. We'd not been seeing so much of each other since I got took on here, we'd just grown apart really – that's how it is.

GIRLFRIEND: Shahid's phone was still off, but sometimes he'd do that. He'd just let the battery run down or leave it off, sometimes for days at a time when he obviously didn't want to talk to anyone.

Actually, at first I was quite annoyed that he hadn't called me to check that I was alright.

I thought 'He must know what's happened…' and 'cos I'd said the night before that I might've been going down to town with my friends today…

I mean, even though he'd told me not to, it doesn't mean I wouldn't have, you know, I'm my own person, I might still have gone...

BROTHER: Time just passed very slowly.

SISTER: And he still didn't call.

BROTHER: No one called.

SISTER: None of us spoke.

BROTHER: None of us wanted to say what we were thinking...

SISTER: I couldn't imagine him not being there for me... I didn't want to think about it.

BROTHER: In our hearts we kept hoping – because we had to keep hoping.

SISTER: The thing is, it gets to the point that you can't think about anything else.

BROTHER: We all knew that the more time passed, the less hope there was of him coming home alive.

At the hospital.

NURSE: A nail bomb is a terrible and inhumane device that can cause dramatic, life-threatening injuries – devastating shrapnel injuries really. The blast sends heavy, sharp, metal objects ripping through tissues and bone...

GIRL 2: The emergency staff were clearly shocked, but doing all they could.

NURSE: I do still have nightmares about the things I saw that day.

SON: Because I was a bit away from the explosion, I was basically OK. There was just some glass in my hair and pockets.

ASSISTANT 1: My mouth was completely dry and my ears were ringing. It actually turned out I'd gone deaf for a short while.

SON: I went to the hospital though, 'cos they thought I might be in shock.

GIRL 2: I was very tearful. I just wanted to get my wound cleaned and stitched and to go home.

SON: I just wanted my Mum.

GIRL 2: I still had that horrible smoke smell in my nostrils.

ASSISTANT 1: I wondered why some people were so badly hurt and not others...

NURSE: There were some people with no injury at all, who were just trembling from head to toe with fear – and when you were close you could feel their terror.

SON: I think part of me already knew... You just get that feeling in the pit of your stomach and you know that something's very, very wrong.

I think that's why I kept asking for her. It was like – I think I thought that by asking for her I was telling myself and everyone else that she was alright, and she was gonna come round the corner at any minute and hug me and ask if I were OK...

NURSE: One girl had suffered awful, horrific injuries to the left side of her body, in particular to her arm and leg. The leg injury was so severe that the lower part of the limb had to be amputated.

GIRL 3: I remember waking up in intensive care. I could still feel my leg, and then I looked down and it wasn't there anymore. I can't describe that feeling... And you just keep looking, you can't help it...

There was a bump in the sheet where my right leg was, and on the left side, where my other leg should have been…nothing.

NURSE: You'll need to have an artificial limb and, I promise, you will learn to walk again.

GIRL 3: She was lovely, but I was just completely distraught.

NURSE: It will take time, and at first you'll only be able to wear it for a couple of hours a day. But we'll help you – you're not going to be going through this on your own…

GIRL 3: It's like, you don't expect something like this is gonna happen when you're out shopping with your friends. You don't expect it…

ASSISTANT 1: I thought:

If the bomb was that close, why aren't I dead?

NURSE: We had a baby with a nail embedded in its head; a child who lost his eye; a young woman with total amnesia who had no idea of what had happened, who she was, where she lived or anything…

GIRL 2: They thought I might have broken my arm, but the x-rays showed it was just badly bruised. They stitched it up, and kept me in for four hours with shock. I knew I was one of the lucky ones. I felt so grateful to be alive.

NURSE: An elderly man had nails lodged in his lungs. His family held a vigil by his bedside but, I'm sorry to say, he died the following day.

ASSISTANT 1: It might sound strange, but I actually feel bad for having survived and having got off so lightly. I keep thinking about that body on top of me – I knew he'd died… I'd felt him die before the emergency services came.

I think he'd have been one of the people trying to reason with Shahid, and must have stayed when I ran away. By being between me and the blast that man saved my life, and I don't even know who he was…

I'll never forget him though.

SPECIAL BRANCH: We had to fully identify those who died at the scene, which isn't pleasant as the force of the blast just sent small bits everywhere.

We made a decision that it wasn't appropriate to put family members through formal identification, because there wasn't really much left for them to identify.

SON: They took me to this room by myself and asked what she'd been wearing.

SPECIAL BRANCH: I'm sorry…

SON: After that I knew I couldn't pretend no more.

SPECIAL BRANCH: (*To audience.*) There'd been her Clubcard impressed in part of the torso.

SON: We never saw the body, but later they gave us back her glasses. Just the frames.

SPECIAL BRANCH: The glass would have come out at the time of the explosion.

SON: That's all we have left of her…

NURSE: All of the victims, their families and friends will have permanent psychological scars, the effects of which cannot be underestimated. The pain will ease with time, but it never fully goes away.

GIRL 3: It's gonna take a long time to get my life back again.

The NURSE has helped GIRL 3 into a wheelchair and now takes her off.

GIRL 3 remains in the wheelchair for the rest of the play.

GIRL 2: When the police talked to me they gave me a forensic bag for my clothes.

ASSISTANT 1: It helps to talk about it. It helps to say what happened.

GIRL 2: I told them what I saw, which weren't much.

ASSISTANT 1: I told them what had happened. I said:

Did he die? Shahid?

I knew him. We were at school together.

He was alright, yeah. Popular…everyone liked him.

He was really good at football. That's what I remember most about him.

He was only eighteen.

I'm eighteen…

It makes you think, don't it?

SPECIAL BRANCH: They held a Cobra meeting in London, involving all the senior politicians. So the Home Secretary was there, and senior representatives from the Army and the Police.

From that they decided to raise the state of alert in the UK to its highest level – which is 'critical' – because inevitably there was the fear of another similar incident or spate of incidents.

ASSISTANT 1: It's like – when it happened in London, when there was the Tube bombs in London – because it was so many hundred miles away it's kind of… I wouldn't say you don't think about it, because obviously it's awful for those people and their tragedies, but you think:

GIRL 2: It's in London…it's not gonna happen to us.

ASSISTANT 1: And I think that's the reality for most people. Until it affects you and comes to your doorstep, you're not really that bothered.

It's an unfortunate thing that really…

NURSE: At first people were very much in shock.

ASSISTANT 2: It hurt the whole community.

ASSISTANT 1: The whole community was grieving.

GIRLFRIEND: Most people were terribly ashamed, you know…they thought of the shame this would bring on our town.

FOOTBALLER: Some people were talking about it, about what had happened.

PCSO: It was too early for anyone to know anything really, the facts. But already the whispers had started.

GIRL 2: And there were those who just kept to themselves, who just wanted to be left alone…

SON: The next day was Mother's Day – it had to be, didn't it? And everywhere it was like you knew there were Mums and kids and families just – having a nice day – spending time together – maybe going out for a meal… Mum's special day…the day you say thank you for being you.

And I couldn't. I could never say that again. And I probably never really said it when she was alive. I never said half the things I meant to say to her, even though I thought it and I did care and I did love her very much…

And there was this little cake that I'd bought her still in my coat pocket. And I'd never be able to give it to her because I was never going to see her, or speak to her, or be with her again.

As the SON leaves it is clear the scene has changed. Two SPECIAL BRANCH OFFICERS – a white male and an Asian female – are now outside a house and heavily armed.

SPECIAL BRANCH: We need to fully identify who this person is. Obviously there'll be witnesses from the scene, CCTV, forensic evidence, DNA…

FEMALE OFFICER: One of the key issues really is to identify possible co-conspirators, which led in this instance to a decision to arrest and detain the perpetrator's family.

SPECIAL BRANCH: An attacked arrest typically involves a large number of resources. We cordoned off the neighbouring streets, and several officers forcibly entered the premises at gunpoint.

FEMALE OFFICER: The place could've been booby-trapped. There could've been someone stood in the front room with another bomb...

Inside the house.

SISTER: The first thing we knew they'd broke down the door.

BROTHER: What are you doing here? What's going on?

SPECIAL BRANCH: *Get down on the floor!*

> *The FEMALE OFFICER repeats the direct commands and instructions (in italics) in Urdu.*

The most important thing is to contain the scene – for the safety of everyone concerned.

SISTER: I was really scared. I thought 'Why is this happening? What do they think we've done?'

SPECIAL BRANCH: *You'll be wearing these white suits.*

BROTHER: (*To audience.*) It's not acceptable for a Muslim to be undressed in the presence of other men.

SPECIAL BRANCH: *We'll need your clothes later. For forensics.*

BROTHER: We were at gunpoint – my parents, my little sister and myself – forced to cover our own clothes with these stupid paper suits so that they could take ours later for evidence...and all the time their prying eyes upon us.

I was so very angry, but I knew I had to keep my cool. If I'd have shown any form of aggression – verbal, physical or otherwise – I didn't like to think of the repercussions on my family.

So I kept the moral high ground. I stayed humble for the sake of my parents, I preserved my dignity as best I could…and just took their crap.

SPECIAL BRANCH: *Right, we're taking you outside.*

SISTER: I thought about our neighbours, watching from behind their curtains.

BROTHER: I could just imagine the photographers…

SISTER: Everyone was gonna be talking and wondering what we'd done…

They go outside.

BROTHER: Outside there was more officers with heavy-duty black guns, which I knew were loaded… It was the longest catwalk I've ever done in my life.

In fairness I will say that they made no attempt to provoke us. They kept their guns pointing down and avoided making eye contact.

SISTER: We were put into these big black cars, and taken straight to Manchester without stopping.

The BROTHER and SISTER are put in separate cells.

SPECIAL BRANCH: They were taken to a high security police station in Manchester, because arrest under TACT – which is terrorist offences really – there are procedural differences right from the arrest phase, through the custody records and having access to various things… It's much more practical to do that in Manchester. They've got trained staff, the custody suites are sealed up – everything's sealed up.

SISTER: That was where they told us about Shahid. I said:

Are you sure? Could it not just have been someone with the same name?

BROTHER: They told us the reason why we'd been arrested and then they set out a plan.

SPECIAL BRANCH: *This what we're gonna be asking about... This is what we're going to be doing...*

BROTHER: I felt like there was no empathy to the fact I'd just lost my brother.

FEMALE OFFICER: We have to make sure that they're aware of their rights, check their welfare, etc.

SISTER: I thought, 'This isn't real. I'm gonna wake up in a minute and none of this will have happened.'

SPECIAL BRANCH: They were all kept separately, in cells. There's access to the Koran and proper resources for prayer. It's absolutely state-of-the-art really...

BROTHER: I mean, look, I understand they've got to question family, but they could have done it at home. Or they could have asked me politely to come down – I would have been happy to do it. But the way they just...it pisses me off.

What have I done wrong? I've done nothing wrong!

FOOTBALLER: When his name came on the news, I didn't know what to think. I had trouble believing it was him to be honest, because I literally thought of the guy I knew.

GIRLFRIEND: I was absolutely stunned – I couldn't even cry. You can't imagine – when it's someone you know... It was like my whole world turned upside down.

FOOTBALLER: They wanted people who'd known him to come forward and give information. But, I mean – talking to the police don't make you too popular round here.

GIRLFRIEND: You think of all those poor people who have been killed or injured, and you know you have to do the right thing:

He was my friend. My boyfriend.

FOOTBALLER: I knew him quite well. We used to be friends...

The GIRLFRIEND and the FOOTBALLER are also taken to individual rooms or cells.

SPECIAL BRANCH: We have to ask precise questions. We can't keep saying 'Did you know anything about it?' ten times over two days. So we had an interview plan.

The whole idea is that we interview one person, come back and review what they've said, and that will influence what we ask person number two or three, and so on...

BROTHER: I said:

I don't know why he's done it. All I know is he's done the wrong thing – it's as simple as that.

SISTER: I said:

He wasn't bad – he was kind and gentle. He used to look out for me... He was always there for me.

BROTHER: Yeah, we were close. I mean, there's only a year between us, so we grew up together.

FOOTBALLER: We were more like brothers than friends, y'know. Since being seven or eight years-old – we was in this junior team together and we just clicked...

GIRLFRIEND: We were together nearly four years... We had made so many plans...

SISTER: I loved him. He meant the world to me.

GIRLFRIEND: I thought we shared everything. I thought there was nothing he couldn't tell me. But I swear I knew nothing about this.

FOOTBALLER: He wasn't racist – I can vouch for that. He was a good friend...he was loyal.

BROTHER: He is – was…he was always able to pick things up with speed – really intelligent lad, y'know.

SISTER: He was going to go to university, he'd got a place at Leeds to do chemistry.

BROTHER: He didn't do so good in his mocks – which Dad was unhappy about – but it was basically because he didn't put in the work.

GIRLFRIEND: I knew he had some problems, I knew things weren't too good at home after his mocks. I just told him things would work out…

BROTHER: I was confident he'd do well when the time came… I've always had that confidence in him.

SISTER: Mum and Dad were really proud – he'd have been the first from our family to go to university.

BROTHER: The thing was, his heart weren't in it – his real passion had always been football. It was his dream to play as a professional.

FOOTBALLER: Oh yeah, he could've, easy. Even as a kid you could tell he had something special.

GIRLFRIEND: I know it meant the world to him. And he got let down.

BROTHER: It was a couple of years back – Man United had these scouts following him and his friend Stuart, 'cos their team was doing really well and they were like the star players.

FOOTBALLER: What happened was they picked me but not Shahid. And I was so caught up in my own excitement that I didn't really consider his feelings. I just made a bit of a joke about it. I said:

Hey pal, it's a pity your surname ain't Smith, innit?

I mean, I didn't mean it in a derogatory way or anything like that, you know, it was meant as a joke.

But Shahid just looked at me and it was like, in that moment he hated me. And he just threw down the ball he were holding and stormed out.

BROTHER: Shahid got the idea into his head that they'd picked Stuart 'cos he was white – now whether that's true or not, I couldn't say.

FOOTBALLER: I never really thought... I honestly don't think that had anything to do with it. I mean, Shahid's best position was on the wing, and we already had that pretty much sorted. I'm sure he'd've got took on by someone else though.

GIRLFRIEND: He felt like a door had been closed in his face.

SISTER: It was his dream, you see. Football was what he lived for.

BROTHER: He packed in the football and had nothing to do, he was just hanging round on the streets looking for something to cling onto, I guess. I knew he was smoking and drinking alcohol for a bit 'cos I could smell it on his breath. It weren't so much a religious thing, but he steered clear when he was playing regular like.

GIRLFRIEND: He used to keep himself in great shape, 'cos his body was his temple he used to say...

FOOTBALLER: I didn't see so much of him after that. I mean, I wasn't around so much, so I wouldn't't've anyway.

GIRLFRIEND: He did change, yeah. He became more sullen, withdrew into himself... It seemed like he always had a frown on his face, whereas before it had always been a smile.

SISTER: He had a lovely smile. His eyes glittered when he was smiling.

GIRLFRIEND: After a while he seemed to get more religious, seemed to...you know, he wore different clothes, and his interests changed. His taste in music and that... Before it was all football, football, football – so I was actually quite pleased at first when he started taking more of an interest in Islam and in world events.

BROTHER: To be honest, before – when things were OK – I was definitely more into Islam than he was, not that I'm a scholar or anything. But I mean, he read the Koran, and he just ticked the box basically. He went to mosque because we all did, and that were it.

GIRLFRIEND: For example, it's like when I'm not at home I don't tend to wear the hijab – I just find it easier to fit in at college without it. And that never used to be a problem.

And then one day he was like 'Why are you moving backwards? What's wrong with you? Maintain your standard!' And I was really shocked, because that just weren't like him at all.

BROTHER: We started to disagree over stuff, which we never had before. I found when we talked about Islam it seemed we had very different ideas, and it got quite heated.

FOOTBALLER: The times we did bump into each other he did seem…a bit different. He was very formal with me, and I was wondering why.

I remember one time I said 'What's up, bro?' And he said 'You're not my bro anymore, I can't talk to you 'cos you're not a Muslim'. And I was like 'Where have you got that from?' And he said it was in the Koran.

And I thought 'What's got into his head? I've not heard that before…'

BROTHER: I was like:

The Koran don't say that – what're you on about?

GIRLFRIEND: There was also this one time when he tried to make me wear the niqab – and I know that's not compulsory and I told him so.

We nearly broke up over that.

BROTHER: I mean, it was stupid really, 'cos neither of us can actually read what the Holy Book says 'cos we don't know Arabic. But suddenly, without studying at the mosque, he seemed to know all about it – and me personally, I didn't think that what he was saying felt right.

GIRLFRIEND: He started to get very angry about what's happening in these far-off countries and about the way the British Government are dealing with Muslims – he didn't agree with it. I mean, neither do I but...

I told him to talk to people about it – and I do know that he tried to. I'm not sure if he went to the mosque – he was never that into the mosque – but I know he spoke to some of the local community leaders, and even our councillor. And he said they weren't interested. He told me that they didn't have no time for him or his views.

SISTER: I heard him going on about how the world was shitting on Islam and shitting on Muslims and how could we just sit on our hands and not want to do something... His language was quite bad, and Dad and Hasan got pretty annoyed with him about that.

BROTHER: The other thing he used to rant about, if anything happened to do with Muslims – like, d'you remember that demo against the soldiers? – and they'd interview someone from some Muslim organisation or other, he'd be like:

'Why do you always talk to them idiots? Why is it always the same bloody faces? They don't know what's going on. They won't talk to us – how can they speak for us? How can they represent our views?'

GIRLFRIEND: I remember when the Tube bombs happened in London and we talked about it. And we were both really shocked and upset, like everyone was. He touched on that again recently, but with a whole new viewpoint – like he really admired what they'd done. He said something along the lines of them standing against the victimisation of Islam

from the terrorists Bush and Blair, and that they'd made
people sit up and take notice of what was going on.

And I said:

What are you talking about? Those guys were brainwashed
and they did the worst thing a Muslim could do. And they
did Islam no favours. And they did Muslims no favours.

He never mentioned it again after that. Probably 'cos he
knew we'd end up fighting over it.

SISTER: There was a lot of hate, hate for everyone. I don't
understand how he came to hate so much.

BROTHER: Looking back I know I should've done more
to question it – I'm angry at myself that I didn't. But
whenever I tried to challenge him he'd just turn nasty, so
in the end I didn't bother. I just put it down to hormones
and things like that.

GIRLFRIEND: But I mean, someone must have influenced him
to think like that – because his thoughts wouldn't have
changed so much all by themselves, would they?

BROTHER: I mean, I know stuff goes on and people get
brainwashed and that, but to be honest I thought, 'There's
nothing going on like that round here.'

You know, if anyone tried to start anything at the mosque,
the imam would have them out in no time – I mean, he's
just not gonna let it happen.

So yeah, I was obviously stupid, but I just put it down to
some hormonal change – I thought it was a phase he was
going through and he was trying to get a reaction. So I'm
ashamed to say I ignored him…

I can't tell you how much I regret that now.

GIRLFRIEND: I'm gonna feel bad for the rest of life that I
could have done something more to help, and I didn't.

I honestly don't think he was part of a group though, I
don't know why I just don't. But if he wasn't and he was
acting on his own without anyone telling him to...what
kind of cold-blooded killer is he?

BROTHER: I mean, ultimately, was he really that stupid?

Look at the Koran, look at its teachings – Islam's about
peace. I know that, I thought he knew that. There's nothing
in there that says it's OK to go and kill yourself or anyone
else for that matter!

SISTER: I guess he just gave up on everyone... I don't know.

PCSO: And it was like, everyone were asking questions.
Everyone wanted to know about his motivation and
possible conspirators – asking why they hadn't had any
intelligence on him, wondering if he could really have
been acting alone.

And I just thought:

But he was like me...

What happens? What was that point? That switch? What
is the switch that flicks someone from thinking logically to
behaving and acting irrationally? The difference between
light and dark...

I mean, what makes people do it?

*The FOOTBALLER and the GIRLFRIEND have been allowed to
leave.*

*During the following speech the SISTER is also released, leaving the
BROTHER alone in his cell.*

SPECIAL BRANCH: Currently we're looking at up to
twenty-eight days, but after an initial review of forty-eight
hours we have to really make a strong case as to why that
person should be kept in custody.

In the case of the parents, who were both quite elderly, the
rationale for keeping them in was not likely to be met. So

they were released, along with the perpetrator's sister, after the initial interviews.

SISTER: They took our passports off us, in case we wanted to flee the country.

SPECIAL BRANCH: The brother had shared a bedroom with the perpetrator, giving them both access to a particular computer which we had seized from the house. Clearly it takes longer to analyse information which is encrypted, so we made a successful case for his continued detention.

BROTHER: It's scary... I mean, I've answered their questions, I've done nothing wrong. And I'm innocent of this – I've got no connection to it whatsoever. And yet there's this fear that I could be detained indefinitely without charge or proof... How can that be right?

PCSO: I understand both sides of it. If the police have reasonable grounds to think that someone might be linked to an atrocity, then of course they've got to investigate.

Because if they do nothing, and they don't take people in and then there's another bombing, everyone's gonna turn round and say:

SOMEONE: Why didn't the police do anything?

PCSO: It's often easier to blame the police. I mean, you've gotta blame somebody...

SISTER: Dad came home after the interview very quiet, he didn't say much. I think he's dealing with it in his own way... I've never seen him cry to be honest.

BROTHER: I mean, I'm not a father, I don't know what it's like to lose a son. But I know what it's like to lose a brother...

SISTER: Mum was the opposite – screaming, pulling her hair...she always heightens things though. She says she was mistreated, but I don't think that's true. I think she was treated exactly the same as the rest of us.

The BROTHER is released.

BROTHER: I was let out later that week – no public apology, no all clear. And people talk don't they, people draw their own conclusions. So I must be guilty, right?

I'm gonna be stuck with this label for a long time.

SISTER: For the first time I can remember Dad didn't go to Friday prayer. Because he was scared. And ashamed.

BROTHER: I couldn't even look at myself in the mirror – I look just like Shahid. I just felt completely paranoid and crap about what had happened to me and to my family. I don't think it will ever really go away.

SISTER: Some people were weirdly sympathetic – trying to be empathetic, if that's a word.

BROTHER: And it would be stupid to say there weren't those who didn't say 'Well done':

INNIT BOY: What was tragic about it? The bro, man, is living a life of luxury in his pad now – he's chilling out. The guy's kicking man. That guy is something to follow.

BROTHER: You know the type I mean – he's got a gold chain, tight jeans, Timberlands…them guys really annoy me.

INNIT BOY: It's being a Muslim, innit? People are picking on us and shit, you know, they're doing the dirty on us. They're killing our brothers over there, innit, in the Middle East and what not, yeah? Nobody gives two shits about them. But when a little bomb attack happens here, everyone's like up in arms and shit.

Well you can't just be rolling over with your tanks and not expect anything. We're not gonna sit back and take it – why should we? We've gotta do exactly what your brother Shahid did. We've gotta stand up and say 'We're not gonna take shit like that, man. We're gonna stand up and fight…' He did right, your bro. This is only one life, man – after this it's heaven.

BROTHER: I said:

> What the hell are you talking about? He went and killed himself and five innocent people. You show me anywhere in the Koran or Hadif where it says that a man can do that and get away with it?

> I was frustrated. I said:

> You don't know how my brother is right now. Don't give me your crap about the seventy virgins and that. My brother is in his grave on his own – you're not there with him. He's going to be questioned by the two black angels, they're going to ask him 'Who is your Lord? Who is your Prophet?' And then they're gonna question him, and I suppose one of the questions is 'Why did you do what you did?' And maybe his answer's gonna be 'It was in the name of Allah…'

> Well, what happens beyond that point I don't know, it's between him and God – but logic tells me that God's probably going to be shaking his head and saying 'Sorry mate, but that was not in My name.'

In the following scene the characters segregate themselves according to their ethnicity.

For the first time in the play it matters that the GIRLFRIEND and GIRL 3 are Asian, and GIRLS 1 and 2 are not.

GIRL 3: When his name first came out, it hurt the whole community.

GIRLFRIEND: He was well known in the area, and people didn't see it coming.

WHITE LAD 1: Straight off you could feel the tensions building up.

GIRL 1: The idea that someone you know would deliberately cause this – cause this suffering…it's just bewildering.

WHITE LAD 2: There's no reason for it to happen. He can't just go and kill innocent people for no reason.

WHITE LAD 1: He'd probably been brainwashed...

GIRL 3: People started to raise questions like – about the Asian thing and the white thing. But our whole community was thinking:

GIRLFRIEND: Why did Shahid kill all these people – including our own community, the Asian community?

GIRL 2: The white lads, the Asian lads – they were all looking for trouble.

ASIAN LAD 1: Everyone was looking for an excuse to start something.

ASIAN LAD 2: Easy round here, innit.

GIRLFRIEND: It was only then that it dawned on me. I thought:

I hope to God people don't expect me to apologise for his actions, because that's not my religion.

ASSISTANT 2: Because people think I'm Asian they think I'm Muslim, so I got a lot of abuse. People were coming up to me saying:

WHITE LAD 3: How come you want jihad against the West?

ASSISTANT 2: And I was like:

Look mate, I dunno – 'cos I'm not a Muslim, I'm a Christian.

WHITE LAD 3: Sure you're a Muslim – you've got the skin ain't you? Your Dad's Asian: you're half-caste.

ASSISTANT 2: Yeah, I'm 'half-caste'.

WHITE LAD 3: So how can you be Christian if you're half-caste?

ASSISTANT 2: Well, hang on… You tell me what a half-caste is.

WHITE LAD 3: A half-caste is a Christian parent and a Muslim parent.

ASSISTANT 2: No, you've got that completely wrong – just because I'm half-caste doesn't make one of my parents a Muslim and one a Christian. I'm half-caste because my Dad was born in Pakistan and he's of Pakistani nationality and my Mum's English. It's nothing to do with your religion, it's to do with where you come from.

It really got me that. They seem to think because you're this colour you're that religion. And it's not.

The OLDER LADS group together. They are clearly psyching themselves up for a fight.

ASSISTANT 2 remains apart from the other characters.

ASIAN LAD 2: All the headlines seemed to say 'Muslims' or 'Islam'.

WHITE LAD 1: 'War on Terror gets Local'.

ASIAN LAD 2: Most people just read the headline and that's it – that's all they need.

WHITE LAD 2: You see a CCTV picture of an Asian lad – you know the rest…

ASIAN LAD 1: Even if you put a whole page of detail, most people don't read it anyway.

ASSISTANT 2: Lack of real information puts things into people's minds, don't it?

Two streets have been created on opposing sides of the stage.

ASIAN LAD 1: Nothing happened at first.

ASIAN LAD 2: It was just this whisper that something might be happening.

WHITE LAD 2: I remember walking to the youth centre, and I was walking down the street and every house I walked past there's people stood outside sort of, you know:

WHITE LAD 3: What's gonna happen tonight?

WHITE LAD 2: That sort of thing. And it was just a little bit...unreal.

ASIAN LAD 1: I'm not entirely sure what the first thing was.

WHITE LAD 2: And then I was at the centre and I got a call from my sister saying:

GIRL 2: Come home. We think there's gonna be a problem, and we'd rather you were here than trying to get home if there was something going on.

As GIRL 2 hangs up the two sides launch at each other. It should be impossible to say who moves first.

RIOT POLICE immediately come between the fighters and attempt to keep both groups apart.

WPC 1: There was a lot of fighting.

ASSISTANT 2: I mean a lot of it was like white groups with the police, Asian groups with the police. There wasn't much white on Asian or Asian on white.

WPC 2: We were in the middle trying to control and push these groups into different areas at different times to try and quell it.

WPC 1: But then what happened is the groups would attack the police:

ASIAN LAD 2: Why can't I go out on my street? This is where I live!

WPC 1: No, you need to stay on that street.

ASIAN LAD 2: I always go out on this fucking street...

WPC 1: It was a no-win situation for us to be honest.

ASIAN LAD 1: You had groups putting windows through, take-aways, taxi firms – you know, where there was a known element from the other faction effectively, they were the target.

WHITE LAD 3: Places got fire-bombed and stuff.

ASSISTANT 2: There was an Indian family who were not Muslim in any way, they were Hindus. They had an off-license/corner shop in a white part of town. And they shut their shop for three days because they were frightened – just because they had brown skin.

WPC 2: That was happening all over.

ASSISTANT 2: I just stayed in. I was afraid – I knew I'd be a target for both sides.

ASSISTANT 2 leaves.

WHITE LAD 1: And there were groups, you know, setting fire to cars…

ASIAN LAD 2: Or they'd get rubbish out, put it all over the street and set fire to that.

GIRL 2: One night, when I was in bed, there were a lot of lads running up and down our street armed with, you know, bits of wood and stones and sticks and things… I was really scared.

The fighting reaches a climax before subsiding.

GIRL 2: Eventually it sort of tapered out.

It was almost as though people just thought:

A & W LADS 1: Right, that's it now.

WHITE LAD 3: We've made our stance.

ASIAN LAD 2: We're not going to do anymore about it.

The fighting has done little to ease tensions and the groups remain segregated.

GIRL 2: But it still seemed that racist people felt they'd got an excuse to make an even bigger deal out of stuff.

GIRL 1: I think they had a point – up to a point.

GIRLFRIEND: The media never shows the fact that the Muslim community condemn violent extremism.

GIRL 3: They don't understand that we're scared of it too.

GIRLFRIEND: They made out like we were all in our houses cheering him on.

SON: They said he was a Muslim and he wanted to kill the non-Muslims.

GIRL 3: They can't say that, they need to say the other side of the story as well.

GIRLFRIEND: It's not about religion. They should write about what drove him to it, or what made him do it.

GIRL 3: And his background and everything...

SON: But my Mum was a Muslim – why did he kill her?

SPECIAL BRANCH: The problem is when the media uses the phrase 'Islamic terrorist' then ninety-nine point nine per cent of Muslims who are not terrorists feel that there's something about being Islamic that's about being a terrorist – or that's what people think.

ASIAN LAD 1: It's about the way people look at you.

GIRLFRIEND: If they give us the look, we give the look back.

ASIAN LAD 1: You feel they've got something in their mind, like:

WHITE LAD 2: He's probably gonna do the same thing...

ASIAN LAD 1: You want to challenge it. You want to say something like:

Do you think I'm a terrorist? What makes you think that?

WHITE LAD 2: It makes you stereotype against people like that. Definitely.

You have it in the back of your mind that the bomber was of that religion, and you have a negative view of it.

SON: If this is my religion, then I hate it.

GIRL 1: I try not to make a judgement on them, but it just seems that now – after it being so close – I'm gonna try and stay away from them.

GIRL 2: But to what extent do you take that? No matter who it is? Our friends? We don't judge them on the way they look...

GIRL 1: I don't think it's possible not to anymore.

GIRLFRIEND: I was sat on a bus and Kirsty wouldn't even sit with me. The bus was packed and the seat was free and she just stood there... I knew exactly why she wouldn't sit with me.

GIRL 3: It's no longer about colour, it's no longer about being Asian – you're a Muslim now.

GIRLFRIEND: It's on the news all the time – 'Muslim, Muslim, Muslim...'

GIRL 3: It just makes people hate us more.

GIRLFRIEND: And then it makes us hate them.

SPECIAL BRANCH: You can't stop it happening. People will twist the words, it's like Chinese whispers. And everything gets exaggerated a bit more and a bit more, making the whole situation worse.

GIRL 1: Someone said that not all Muslims believe that, but most of them do. It's what they teach in the mosques and stuff.

GIRL 2: You don't know that...

GIRL 1: It's obvious. Why d'you think it says it in the papers? I think we should have seen it coming really – we could've prevented it.

I mean, if this is how they're gonna behave then they should just go back to their own country – 'cos this is just ridiculous.

GIRL 3: We feel like we're gonna get kicked out of England – and we've got nowhere to go 'cos we was born here and so was our parents...

But everyone says there's been more terrorism happening since Muslims have been in England.

GIRLFRIEND: What about the IRA? Don't they care about them?

ASIAN LAD 1: The IRA aren't 'Christian terrorists' so I don't understand how they can turn round and say it's the Muslim people – 'cos don't they know there's different types of Muslims? There's about – let's see – seventy-two, seventy-three different types of Muslims...

SON: I don't want to be a Muslim anymore.

ASIAN LAD 1: You get bad apples in every community, not just ours...

GIRLFRIEND: It doesn't matter what we do, does it? Whatever we do is gonna be wrong. If we do something right it's gonna be wrong. If we do something wrong it's gonna be wrong.

ASSISTANT 2: People play on it as well though, because it's become a power thing now. I saw a group of lads having a disagreement, and an Asian lad turned round and said to a white lad:

ASIAN LAD 2: You need to shut your fucking mouth or I'm gonna come and bomb you and your family.

ASSISTANT 2: And they're using it as a power kick, it's like a 'you're next' type of thing. You know, when you hear them saying:

ASIAN LAD 2: You hear me? You fuck with us and we're gonna get you?

ASSISTANT 2: It's like they're boasting about it, and it saddens me because people have died – innocent people – what is there to boast about? And they don't understand that by saying that, them white kids are gonna think:

WHITE LAD 1: Oh, so it is the Muslims. You're just saying exactly what we think.

ASSISTANT 2: So instead of ignoring it, or saying:

Why are you calling me a terrorist?

It turns out that he's accused him and he's accused him back. And he goes home thinking:

WHITE LAD 1: Yeah, you clearly are terrorists.

ASSISTANT 2: And he goes home thinking:

ASIAN LAD 2: You're just white trash.

ASSISTANT 2: And that's how it is. Unless they stop saying it – even for a joke – it's just gonna end up like that.

GIRLFRIEND: I guess it works both ways.

GIRL 2: There's fear on both sides.

GIRL 1: Fear is the word.

GIRL 3: It makes you feel like…it's a massive barrier. And we need to get rid of it.

PCSO: Now, I've not been to an Islamic school. I used to go to the mosque, and I hated it 'cos all I saw was this mosque man. And you know what it's like when you're being told to do something and you don't understand it…

So when I finished the Koran I was like:

Great, I can go home now – I don't want to go back to the mosque.

I mean, I know the basics – you're supposed to pray five times a day, do pilgrimages, fasting, be nice to people and all that – but that were it really. 'Cos I'd read the Holy Book in Arabic – which is the normal way – and I don't understand Arabic.

But after this business with the bomb and all of what the media were saying, I think a lot of us started to think:

GIRLFRIEND: That's not me – that's not what I believe.

ASIAN LAD 1: I didn't think Islam was like that…

GIRL 3: Why did I study it if I don't know what it means?

PCSO: So you don't think what they're saying is true, but how can you challenge it if you don't have the answers yourself? You can't educate people if you don't have the knowledge yourself…

And I was going into work and my colleagues were asking me:

WPC 2: What's this jihad?

WPC 1: What's your Holy Book say about what he did?

WPC 2: D'you support this Holy War?

PCSO: And I didn't have any answers, which I found quite shaming. I'm here calling myself a Muslim, but I don't know hardly anything about my religion.

What I did – I got hold of an English version of the Koran, from an Islamic bookshop, and I read that and started to understand it.

It's like anything else, you can take one line out of context and twist it to make it mean what you like – and people do that with the Bible too, don't tell me that they don't. But in order to really understand the message, you obviously have to place that line in the context of the whole – and also in the context of the life of the Prophet, that's really important.

So I went out and found out the answers to the questions of my colleagues. Because of what the media were saying. And because I didn't believe what they were saying. About jihad and Holy War and all that. And what I found out – it's totally the opposite, it's peace. Islam means peace.

SPECIAL BRANCH: That's why I became a Muslim. It was after the London Tube bombings: 7th July 2005. My girlfriend was studying in London at the time and missed the second bomb by a matter of minutes…

But afterwards, when there was all this Islamic phobia being stirred up in the press and that, I thought:

I don't think that's right that. I can't believe a religion really teaches those things…

So I went out and researched it for myself as well. And realised not only that I'd found something really special that's been misrepresented and misinterpreted, but that it was how I wanted to live my life:

And yeah, basically Islam's a peaceful religion which completely condemns any form of extremist views, terrorist views, anything like that. Our Prophet, peace be upon him, taught that it's not right to kill anyone including yourself. Only God can take life.

But if Islam is misunderstood, then I think jihad is even more misunderstood. I read in the paper recently – a quality paper, not a tabloid – that the Koran justifies jihad, the Koran says that if you die in the name of Islam it's the best way to die. A completely misquoted verse – completely misquoted:

Jihad basically means struggle. And the main part of that's your internal struggle against those things that prevent you from doing the things you should be doing – for example, jealousy. It's got nothing to do with the War on Terror!

PCSO: And the only way you can become a martyr is if you die in a Holy War, but that's gotta be declared by the highest cleric. Nobody's declared Holy War, so to fight for the cause of Iraq in this country – or even America – and to kill innocent people, that is killing innocent people. You're not killing George Bush who's done that; you're not killing Tony Blair who's done that… Just because they've done it, don't make it right for you to!

So if you hear somewhere 'Kill the non-believers!' you know what – read the rest of the story, mate. Don't just do what the press do and what the BNP do and take extracts out of context and use them for your own ends. I mean, it's pretty clear they're no experts on the Koran!

I mean, a Muslim can't be a terrorist. It's just…obvious.

SPECIAL BRANCH: I find it sad that we never really hear about what the major faiths have in common – you know, everyone always focuses on the differences. If a Muslim were to say to a Christian 'You're a non-believer, you're not a Muslim' that's actually wrong because they are Muslims – they believe in God. And it's also the case that by being a Muslim you're automatically a Christian and a Jew. Not a lot of people know that…

PCSO: Even the atheists. I mean, I watched this video on You Tube and there was this scholar who said that even an atheist is half way to becoming a Muslim.

SPECIAL BRANCH: How come?

PCSO: Because they say the first part of the declaration of faith. We say:

MUSLIM: There is no god but Allah and Muhammad is His servant and messenger.

PCSO: They say:

ATHEIST: There is no God...

PCSO: I think that's funny, that's pretty good – all they gotta do is complete the other half and they're there!

The GIRLS are back at college.

GIRL 1: Things will never be the same. There's no point in pretending otherwise.

GIRL 2: It's very difficult to talk about it afterwards. I mean, it's just... I don't know, I just don't want to go out, I don't want to do things anymore. I mean, how do you move on after everything that's happened?

GIRL 3: The only way we can move on is by – not putting it behind us, but not keep bringing it up every time someone says a wrong word against us.

GIRLFRIEND: We've got to talk to them. We've gotta try and explain... We'll just explain how it is – and if they can't take it we'll leave it.

GIRL 2: I find it hard now to go and talk to them...

GIRL 1: It's not that I'm frightened, it's just that...if we go to talk to them, we don't know what their reaction would be. So I'm kind of, not scared but...

GIRLFRIEND: I mean, everyone's reaction is bad, but it's worse when it's your friends or, like people who should understand you and who mean something to you.

GIRL 3: And then when college re-opened and it was lunch.

GIRL 2: It just happened:

The two groups notice each other.

GIRL 1: Anna, hurry up!

GIRL 2: I thought we had twenty minutes.

GIRL 1: Just...be quick.

GIRLFRIEND: Don't leave on our account.

GIRL 1: Anna, come on!

GIRL 2: I have to wash my hands.

GIRLFRIEND: I didn't think hygiene was your thing.

GIRL 3: Did you have to say that?

GIRLFRIEND: It's just that they were leaving – on our account, because we were even there. It made me feel like dirt and I just said:

Look, just 'cos he did it – that's one person... It doesn't mean we'll all do it.

GIRL 3: It's not what we believe – it's not in the Koran.

GIRL 1: That's not what the papers say.

GIRL 2: Why would they lie to us?

GIRL 3: Why would we lie to you?

GIRLFRIEND: Look, from what I see, there's a very small amount of people who say they're speaking 'on behalf of the Muslim community' when actually they're not.

GIRL 3: Didn't you hear what happened to me? And that Muslim lady who died? How do you think that family are feeling now?

GIRLFRIEND: But when a Muslim tries to say something sensible, no one wants to listen – apart from Muslims. And if that only stays in the Muslim community, it's not helping nobody, is it? I mean, you could've at least asked us about it.

GIRL 1: Yeah but why is it always a one-way thing? Why is it always about you? And us having to ask you? You've not tried to talk to us about it either.

GIRLFRIEND: We've had things to cope with, you know.

GIRL 1: And we were in it too! I watched it all. I saw everything happen – when I was outside I saw everybody…coming out.

GIRL 2: I saw things that were just… I just can't… And I was just trying to do my job… And there was people dying in ways that you just don't want to even… And nobody even came to help them.

GIRLFRIEND: And then there was this silence 'cos obviously, you know – that made me think. It's just, sometimes you don't think.

GIRL 1: I dunno, I just wanted them to leave, 'cos it still seemed like there was a lot of tension between us.

GIRL 3: I understand where they're coming from. I mean, I would if I was in their shoes, I'd be scared. I still am actually, 'cos it happened to me too…

But we're supposed to be friends, and the point of friendship is that your friends should come first. So I just said:

We shouldn't let our religion come between us.

GIRL 1: Yeah, but… Look, I'm sorry, I've just got to say this – I know it sounds bad, but I really hate it when, like…last year it's all Happy Eid, Happy Hanukka, and I'm fine with that – but then it's like 'Oh, you can't say Happy Christmas because it's offensive to Muslims.' Like…well you should be tolerant of us if you want us to be tolerant of you!

GIRL 3: But I love Christmas – we have a Christmas dinner and everything in my family. That's just another example of ignorant people stirring things up.

GIRLFRIEND: You know, what's happened's happened – we just have to try and get through it now. And maybe we can be friends again…

GIRL 2: (*After a pause.*) I'd like that.

GIRL 1: After that we did start to talk again. It was, like, gradual, but sort of deeper...

GIRL 2: We asked each other about things we wouldn't have done before.

GIRL 1: And it was both ways. 'Cos even though we're all from round here and British and that – we are from different cultures and have different traditions. I sort of ignored it before – you feel a bit rude asking – but once you feel it's ok...and it's actually kind of interesting.

GIRL 3: It's not just them, it's us as well. They need to realise that not all Muslims are the same, just like we should realise that not all whites are the same.

GIRLFRIEND: But I thought you supported the Iraq War and all that?

GIRL 1: Well, some people did, but it's not all of us.

GIRL 2: We know it was illegal – and loads of people marched against it.

GIRL 3: If the government had listened to them it would never have happened.

GIRL 1: We all know that...

GIRL 2: I personally think that George Bush and Tony Blair should be tried for war crimes, 'cos they're terrorists too.

GIRL 1: I guess it's the same really, isn't it?

GIRL 3: We shouldn't be fighting the politicians' war, y'know...

GIRL 2: And what Shahid did hasn't made any difference to them.

GIRLFRIEND: Just to us...

The GIRLS remain in position as the other characters enter separately to speak their lines.

Ideally the entire cast should be on stage by the final speech.

SON: I still don't understand. Nothing's gonna bring her back.

ASSISTANT 2: I haven't gone back to my job…they've offered us counselling, but right now I can't do it.

PCSO: I just hope lessons can be learnt from this: not to take religion – or anything else – to the extreme… I mean, it even says that in the Koran.

SISTER: I still pray for my brother. Because there was a part of him, and I still believe there is a part of him that…that is good. It's just been buried by whatever influenced his mind.

BROTHER: I weep for him. How could he think that this was noble or just?

ASSISTANT 1: At the memorial service I lit a candle for those who didn't make it… And another in thankfulness for being alive.

FOOTBALLER: We held a minute's silence for the victims – a lot of clubs round here did that – (*A long pause.*) And I just thought back over everything we went through together and wondered how it could've come to this.

Lights slowly fade through the following speech.

SPECIAL BRANCH: On March 13th 2010 Shahid Hussain, an angry and confused young British man, committed an appalling atrocity resulting in the loss of six lives including his own, and devastating our local community.

To call this an Islamic crime would be incorrect, there was nothing Islamic about it. If Mr Hussain believed he was killing and dying in the name of his religion, he was sadly mistaken.

He was brought up a Muslim. But although his love of his faith was sincere his knowledge was not deep – leaving him vulnerable to potential radicalisation. It is clear he was radicalised, that he was given distorted interpretations of the Koran, and we have evidence to suggest this was the work of an individual, not an organised group.

Be assured we will do all we can to find this person and bring him to justice. In the meantime, please, be vigilant. And don't become his next victim.

Black out.

The first production of this play was followed by a structured forum session between the audience and an actor playing SHAHID.

Having established that events in the play haven't yet taken place, the focus was on addressing Shahid's current understanding of Islam and his personal concerns with British foreign policy. The audience was asked to correct his religious misconceptions and to suggest a range of practical and non-violent ways in which Shahid could put his point-of-view across, with the intention of changing his future actions.

Whilst this is not essential, it did provide a useful opportunity for audience members representing a wide cross-section of communities to discuss a range of issues raised by the play with each other and initiated some very positive local dialogues that may not otherwise have occurred.

WWW.OBERONBOOKS.COM

 Follow us on www.twitter.com/@oberonbooks
& www.facebook.com/OberonBooksLondon

Printed in the USA
CPSIA information can be obtained
at www.ICGtesting.com
LVHW020748181024
794056LV00008B/702